CW01651740

Calm Your Worry Warrior...

and Allow Your True Self To APPEAR!

By

Sandra Hughes

2nd edition

First Published in 2021 by Mabel &Stanley Publishing.

Please note: the information in this book is intended as a guide to improve wellbeing. It is not intended to replace medical advice. **If you, or anyone you know, requires urgent mental health support please refer to your GP or local Mental Health crisis support teams.**

Other support and advice can be found from other places including:

Samaritans; https: //www.samaritans.org/ or call 116 123
Mind: https://www.mind.org.uk/

Chapter One

Why have you decided to read this book?

Perhaps you picked up this book because there was something in the title that sounded appealing to you; maybe you already recognise that you have a Worry Warrior that you would, indeed, prefer to be calm.

Or was it that you realised your true self may be hiding somewhere in the background, meaning you're not always living life as you would like to?

Or maybe you want to discover what *is* a Worry Warrior and why anyone would want to calm it.

Whatever your reason for choosing to read this book, in doing so, you will begin a journey of self-discovery, one that could be the beginning of a whole new, exciting chapter of your life.

This may sound like a rather over-enthusiastic outcome from reading such a little book; however, within these pages, I am offering you an insight into the tried and tested strategies that I have delivered in workshops, retreats and individually with clients that have resulted in the most remarkable shifts in people's lives.

If you wonder if this book could make a difference, consider the following questions; if there is a yes anywhere in the list, then definitely read on!

- Have you noticed that you spend more time worrying about what's happening around you than enjoying it?
- Do you spend too much time worrying about future events, so there is no time to feel excited about them?
- Or perhaps you go over and over in your mind worrying about what's already happened even though you know you can't change the past?
- Maybe you worry about what others think of you, worrying if what you have done is right.
- Does it feel your responsibility to sort out everyone else's problems?

- Do you feel overwhelmed with the feeling that it always has to be you that sorts things out?
- Are you often preparing for the worst to happen, constantly thinking of solutions 'just in case' it does?
- Is the prospect of doing something new challenging for you? You might even avoid it because it all feels too much.
- Does it feel difficult to say no, even when you know it's better for you if you do?
- Do you have any fears or phobias that get in your way of doing things you would like to?

If any of these things feel familiar, rest assured you are not alone. I see these challenges arise repeatedly in many clients I work with.

All are indicators that an overactive 'Worry Warrior' is likely to be present, jumping into action, getting in the way of you being who you are truly meant to be.

The situations above may all seem quite challenging, and perhaps we might never consider doing anything about changing them; maybe thinking, "Why do I need help? I've done well getting this far, so why would I change?"

However, when we recognise that feelings connected to these situations, such as apprehension, overwhelm, panic, fear, guilt, anxiety, shame, embarrassment, low confidence and poor self-esteem, can all be connected to our Worry Warrior being present, then discovering how to change things and be free of these feelings may seem a lot more interesting.

Perhaps you might believe that feeling this way 'is just part of who I am', and you may never have even considered that there is another way for things to be.

However, what's important to recognise is that this anxious state is not 'who you *are,*' it's actually 'who you have *become*', and it is quite possible to change things; to discover the real you that sits behind your Worry Warrior.

Recognising an overactive Worry Warrior means it's possible to bring all sorts of new dimensions to your life, more calmness, more happiness and also improved health.

Many people don't recognise the negative impact that living life in Worry Warrior mode can bring.

Our stress response is activated when our mind is set to Worry Warrior Mode. This can be helpful for short periods to get us out of difficult situations, but when this becomes a persistent feature and our stress response is switched on continuously, it can have long-term adverse effects on our physical and emotional health.

It can mean that we find ourselves living a different path to the one we might choose, as the Worry Warrior hijacks our thoughts, feelings and actions.

In addition, the presence of a Worry Warrior and the resulting overactive stress response can also bring problems to our physical health.

We may recognise the connection between the Worry Warrior and anxiety and depression, but it may come as a surprise to realise that having an overactive stress response present can trigger many chronic physical health conditions too.

This includes conditions such as IBS, migraines, high blood pressure, fibromyalgia, chronic pain, hormonal imbalances, cancer and heart disease, to name just a few.

Consequently, taming the Worry Warrior is perhaps more important than you may have realised.

It's a message I have become so passionate about sharing because it can have such devastating effects if left unaddressed.

It's a concept so often ignored, perhaps, because we don't realise the size of the problem or maybe just because it feels too complex a problem to solve.

However, once you have read this book, I hope you will see that it is possible; there is a way, a tried and tested approach that really does work, and now it's your turn to discover what a difference it could make for you.

Before we go on, let me explain my journey and what's brought me to a place where I can confidently share a successful recipe to Calm Your Worry Warrior and help you live a happier, healthier and more fulfilling life.

My Journey

My journey of helping people 'feel better' started at a very young age; my childhood hero was Nurse Nancy from the comic Twinkle, who always found a way to make things better. My favourite toy was my medical case, ready for any doll or teddy who might need care.

At age ten, I decided I wanted to be a physiotherapist, having discovered there was such a job from a school friend whose mother ran the local physiotherapy department.

My plan became a reality when I started training as a physiotherapist in 1984 at Kings College Hospital, London, and I went on to have the privilege of working in many different clinical settings, in the NHS, in the Private sector and also with sports teams.

I then went on to manage physiotherapy departments and also moved on to develop healthcare services as a Commissioning manager in a Primary Care Trust.

But whatever role I had, my focus has always been on inspiring positive change to improve health and wellbeing and to help individuals reach their full potential.

I enjoyed making a difference in people's lives, and seeing many clients return to full fitness was very satisfying. However, what became apparent in my role as a Physio was that some clients' symptoms weren't resolving entirely with a traditional physical therapy approach.

Amongst this group, a common theme emerged for me; these clients were all living life with their stress response set to high alert.

I wanted to be able to make a difference with these clients and decided that further training in psychological therapies was the next step for me.

I trained as a Clinical Hypnotherapist, Psychotherapist and BWRT (BrainWorking Recursive Therapy) Practitioner; I read about this subject as much as I could and connected with as many specialists in this field as I was able to.

Bringing all this knowledge together, I developed a business that addresses both emotional and physical well-being based on the fact that these elements are intrinsically linked as part of our body's natural physiology.

In addition to my professional interest, more personal reasons sparked my interest in the body and mind connection.

When my daughter developed anxiety and depression as a teenager, we gradually began to recognise the connection between her emotional state and some physical problems she had experienced as a young child.

The death of a friend appeared to be one of the triggers for anxiety and depression developing, but, in hindsight, we recognised that she had been living with her stress response highly activated for a very long time.

We realised that a severe allergy and also a chronic pain condition that she had developed as a younger child were, in fact, physical signs that she was under stress, her young mind not being able to understand or express how she felt.

Thankfully, through the support of an amazing Therapist and a wonderful homeopath to help her allergies, she has been able to work through those difficulties and has gone from strength to strength; now much more aware of how to manage her system's response to stress.

My journey, both professionally and personally has shaped my mission.

From a professional perspective, I want my clients to receive the most appropriate care there is, using scientific facts to optimise their emotional and physical wellbeing.

But also, as a fellow human being, I want to share this message out there with everyone!

Things can be different; your emotional needs are important and addressing them can completely change the path of your life, no matter what age you are when you discover this.

I've worked with clients from teens to eighty years old, it's never too soon or too late to act on this.

It's a message once heard you can't ignore, when you appreciate that there is a different way for things to be, why would you choose anything else?

Deciding to calm your Worry Warrior can bring all sorts of opportunities, some that have been long wished for and others quite unexpected.

Julia was one of my physio clients who had recognised her Worry Warrior was always at the forefront of her life but believed that she had 'everything covered.' She dealt with challenges in life by being super organised and constantly one step ahead of everything.

However, what she hadn't realised was that her ongoing back pain and sciatica were connected to the stress that the worrying created.

By working with me she was able to let go of the stress and worry she had previously lived with and also discovered that her pain considerably improved as a result. I will explain more about the connection between pain and our stress response later in the book.

Julia's confidence improved and she was amazed to find that she was successful in finding her dream job, something she had coveted for many years.

Jane was another client who came to me because she recognised that stress was getting in the way of her enjoying life. She recognised that she was missing out on enjoyable time with her family because all of her attention was directed toward work. She previously had thought that work was busy and stressful but discovered that the pressure she felt, was arising from the need to prove her worth.

Jane's perception of her value as a person was so connected to success at work, she found it difficult to switch off from this.

After working together, Jane was able to shift some of the unhelpful beliefs which were behind this problem, resulting in her being able to take a more balanced approach at work and noticing a huge improvement in her family life too.

These are just a couple of examples of clients who have sought help from me as they recognised that life was becoming increasingly difficult. They decided that it was time to do something different before their situation escalated into a crisis.

I hope that this book will provide a possible way forward for others in similar situations. It aims to help those with a life restricted by anxiety, self-doubt and overthinking, bringing a simple message that it *is* possible to make a change once you discover how to 'Calm Your Worry Warrior .....and Allow Your True Self to APPEAR!'

Chapter Two

Why do I worry?

Understanding our Stress Response

One of our brain's primary functions is to keep us safe; its most powerful automatic function is to react to what it perceives as danger around us.

When the brain recognises that we are in a 'dangerous' situation it will trigger 'protection mode,' setting off a series of events in our body which help us deal with that perceived danger.

The brain prepares us for either fighting the dangerous situation, running away from it or freezing, just like any animal would when threatened.

This is called our Fight, Flight or Freeze reaction.

In this protection mode or 'stress response' we may notice a series of *automatic physiological* responses that occur in our bodies and which are designed to help us deal with the threat.

You will probably recognise these physiological effects when you are in a frightening situation. Our heartbeat races faster, our breathing becomes quick and shallow, our hands sweat, our nerves become more sensitive, our digestive system either shuts down or empties and our muscles tense up ready to either fight, run from, or freeze in the face of the threat. This also impacts our thoughts, shutting down our rational thought processing, and moving into autopilot.

This generally proves to be a really helpful way to keep us safe and, once we recognise that the danger has passed, our 'alarm systems' will reset as our 'rest and recovery response' is activated and we can carry on our merry way.

However, the problems arise when the stress response remains activated, and a Worry Warrior within us stays on patrol permanently, flooding us with worrying thoughts, and uncomfortable feelings, stopping us from doing things we might like to.

The Amazing Brain

To understand how this can happen, let's take a look at some of the basic principles of how our brain functions.

The brain receives information from all around us and from many different sources, e.g., eyes, ears, nose, touch etc. It also receives information from within our body, helping to regulate our body's function.

The brain is a bit like a computer. It stores incoming information and then processes this by comparing it with past experiences to work out its significance. It then decides what information is relevant and will automatically send out the instructions for the relevant response, based on our past experiences.

Over 80% of what we do are automated responses; our brain just wouldn't have the capacity or the speed to consciously deal with all we do each day.

So, just like a computer, once a certain programme has been installed, it will continue to provide the same response each time that programme is switched on.

We store this 'data' in what are called neural pathways. The brain is made up of millions of nerve cells connected by nerve fibres, creating a very complex circuitry with thousands of different connections.

Messages in our brain are sent along these fibres, or neural pathways, and for every different message, there will be a different sequence of firing of these nerves.

Each neural pathway is a blueprint for us to respond in any given situation, generally helping us through our day without having to think about the minute details of everything we do.

Our brain's role is to compare and filter new experiences and to identify situations that could potentially be dangerous for us. For the majority of the time these learned patterns are really helpful for us, keeping us safe and learning new useful skills.

When storing 'data' of experiences, the higher the emotion attached to that experience, the more significant our brain perceives it to be, and the more likely it will store it for our future use. So, if we experience something that we feel is a danger or a threat to us, which elicits an intense emotion, the brain holds onto that for future reference, capturing in that memory everything little detail associated with experience.

If, in the future, we encounter what the brain feels is a similar situation, an automatic response will be triggered resulting in all the thoughts, feelings and actions that were part of the original situation, regardless of its significance to us in the present day.

These automatic responses happen so fast that they occur even before we are consciously aware of them. This is why sometimes we may find ourselves feeling uncomfortable in certain situations, or perhaps behaving in a way we would rather not, even though rationally we can see no reason why we should.

As a result, we may feel like it is out of our control perhaps feeling like there is no other way to be. This shapes the belief of who we feel we are and can continue to influence our future expectations.

Our brain is made up of a 'map of memories,' or neural programmes, created from experiences of our past. This map is running constantly in the background of our conscious awareness, informing our core beliefs and values about 'our world', directing our expectations for the future, and shaping our thoughts, emotions and actions in the present.

As discussed, most of the time this automatic process is really helpful, the brain working in such a way to protect us and to help us through our day without having to process every thought or action.

However, problems can arise when these programmes continue to run even though they are not relevant to us in the present.

Those reactions and responses may have been helpful in the past, but may now be out of date, resulting in us responding in a way that we may not need or want.

These programmes influence our perception of the present world. What feels real is only real because our brain tells us so. This is why people react differently to the same situation; we have all had a different backdrop of experiences, seeing situations from different places, and therefore perceiving our worlds in different ways.

So, even if we consciously know something not to be a threat, an old unhelpful programme can tell us that it could be a problem and can trigger our stress response into action.

The more unhelpful programmes that are running in our unconscious, the more they fill up our 'Stress Bucket', meaning the more likely we are to be in Worry Warrior mode, with our stress responses being pushed into overdrive.

When our stress response is activated, we are less able to make rational decisions because most of what we are doing is driven out of fear or protection.

The uncomfortable thoughts and feelings that come attached to the unhelpful programmes get in the way of us being who we want to be, so when we start to look at eliminating the unhelpful programme, we can begin to empty the Stress Bucket and so Calm our Worry Warrior.

It all sounds so simple, which it is! Although there is a lot of complicated science behind it, we just need to understand that the brain has an amazing capacity to learn new things and with a tried and tested strategy to follow in this book, it is possible to begin that process.

What I love about the work I do is seeing the amazement from clients when firstly they understand that it *is* possible to change. It's even more wonderful to see their relief when they actually make those changes; literally transforming their life in ways they had never imagined possible.

Chapter Three

My Worry Warrior has got me to where I am now, so why change?

Some clients come to me ready to make a change because they have had enough of feeling exhausted or overwhelmed; they are fed up living life in such a high gear and they recognise that there is a different way to be, they just don't know how to get there.

But there are also many people living in the shadow of their Worry Warrior who don't recognise that there is a different way to live life; believing that worrying is the way that they cope with life.

"It has helped me get through life so far, so why change things?", is something I may be asked. This may seem a fair question, but when we explore the impact that the constant stress mode can have on us, it becomes so much clearer that living life with our Worry Warrior on high alert is definitely not good for us at all!

If our Worry Warrior is always present it can have a negative impact on the quality of our mood, our health and how we live our life.

Stress and its Influence on Our Mood

Many of us may be familiar with the feeling of stress that arises when we have had a challenging day. Our stress response can be activated when we are under pressure to get everything done and this can be helpful in the short term, pushing us forward to get things sorted.

But, if our stress response is switched to Worry Warrior Mode permanently, it can result in us living life from a very negative place. If our past experiences have resulted in our Worry Warrior taking over on a daily basis, we may find life blighted by many unhelpful and very uncomfortable feelings such as self-doubt, overwhelm, anger, sadness, guilt or overthinking.

Feeling negative emotions is completely normal - it's part of being human; we are able to experience a whole spectrum of emotions. But, when our Worry Warrior is switched on permanently, we may find that we get stuck in a pattern of these unhelpful feelings and thinking, constantly feeling we can't escape from them and finding that this significantly impacts our emotional well-being.

When we experience these feelings for so long it is possible that we actually begin to believe that they are part of who we are. We create an expectation that this is how life is, believing that this is who we are rather than recognising this is who we have become due to past situations we have experienced.

Living life in worry mode can be pretty miserable, it can spoil enjoyable times, forcing us to be on the permanent lookout for what might go wrong, along with adverse impacts on many other areas of our lives too.

The Impact of Stress on How We Act

As previously mentioned, many of our daily actions are driven by our unconscious processing and, for the most part, this is helpful but on occasions, it's not; out-of-date programmes can bring back old memories, and create unhelpful thoughts, feelings and behaviours.

For example, if in the past we experienced something that resulted in us feeling vulnerable, given a similar situation, we may find ourselves acting in our Worry Warrior Mode, displaying 'fight flight or freeze' responses. In fact, if our present-day self was able to process the situation calmly and unhindered by past experience, we may rationalise this and deem such an extreme response unnecessary.

In such a scenario, where we feel this vulnerability, we might shout or argue (fight), take ourselves away from the situation (flight), or perhaps be completely blindsided by the whole thing and appear like a rabbit in headlights (freeze).

All of these responses may not be what we might choose were we able to calmly review the situation, think about an appropriate response and carry that out in a considered way. In such a situation our Worry Warrior rushes to take over, trying to protect us and, by doing so, not delivering the best outcome for us.

In many situations, we may develop coping strategies to get around these unhelpful programmes but very often they aren't helpful either!

What can happen is that we learn new activities or behaviours that create a numbing effect for the uncomfortable feelings or thoughts that certain situations trigger within us.

These include scenarios such as overworking, over-exercising, over and under-eating, over-giving, and excessive drinking, to name just a few. These may give us a short-term 'hit' but will create long-term negative effects within us.

We may not be aware that these coping behaviours arise because our Worry Warrior is driving us to take this action, to help us avoid the uncomfortable feelings, although we may notice that they are very difficult to move away from.

Generally, we are not often aware of the reasons behind these actions, for example, we may not realise that overworking can arise from the need for perfection, where our Worry Warrior is fearful of getting things wrong. In this example, we may believe that we are simply a perfectionist - this is who I am, and we don't acknowledge that there is a fear behind this behaviour.

Unfortunately, there is a limited lifespan to any coping strategy; beneath the surface, our Worry Warrior is at play, its long-term presence resulting in detrimental impacts on us. Too often we do not realise the effects of these unhealthy strategies until those unhelpful effects show up.

Even when we are aware that we want to change things, due to the automatic nature of our Worry Warrior impact it can be a challenge to make those changes.

Some might say that we have little free will to make choices about what we do because every decision we make will have been dictated, to some degree, by our past experiences and the beliefs and expectations that were created.

Our brain will always compare any situation it encounters to what's gone before and as such, will influence our decisions. If we do want things to be different, it's important to ensure that the beliefs and expectations that run those programmes are ones which will help us get to where we want to be in life.

It's a bit like making sure that your satnav map is up to date, if you don't then you can end up somewhere you don't want to be!

Calming our Worry Warrior is certainly the first place to start if we want to make permanent changes to these kinds of scenarios, and to bring us more choice in how we respond to situations around us.

Physical Changes Associated with Stress

Not only does the persistent presence of our Worry Warrior influence our mood and our actions it has a negative effect on our physical body and our health too.

When our brain perceives danger, a hormone called adrenalin is produced. This in turn triggers a chain of events via our sympathetic nervous system that results in the changes that are required to protect us.

Our heart and breathing rates increase, bringing more oxygen into our bodies. Our muscles prepare for action by contracting (tightening up). Our digestive system either shuts down or empties, and our nervous system goes into high alert ready to detect more danger.

If the stress is perceived to continue another hormone, cortisol, will take over the job from adrenalin; this keeps the stress response active, ready for us to fight, flight or freeze in the face of the danger we believe to be present.

This is an amazingly fine-tuned system, our body automatically reacting to messages from our brain to keep us safe. However, it is only designed to work for short periods, until the danger passes. The cortisol levels will then drop, which in turn activates a different sequence of events via our parasympathetic nervous system and returns us to a comfortable resting state.

This process generally serves us well, however, problems can arise if the triggers of stress continue; cortisol levels remain high and our systems are put into overdrive, our Worry Warrior never giving us a chance to rest.

If this persists over a long period, our body is then in a constant state of high alert and this can have long-term effects on our physical health. Just like always driving a car at high speed - never taking your foot off the gas- eventually, this will have an impact on how the car functions.

Health Problems Associated with Stress

When physical symptoms are present, it is always important to have a medical assessment to rule out any serious underlying pathology, but it's also important to consider whether our stress response may be contributing to physical symptoms in any way.

It is so important to recognise that, if our Worry Warrior is constantly active, it could be harming our health; another important reason to address the stress we may be experiencing.

Persistent adrenalin surges can cause damage to our blood vessels, raising blood pressure and increasing the risk of *stroke and heart attack*.

The changes that occur in the digestive system when we are under stress can result in long-term *digestive issues* such as irritable bowel syndrome, which can be associated with bloating, painful cramps, upset stomach and constipation.

Many *sleep disturbances* can also be associated with stress; as our mind tries to address our worries while we are sleeping, resulting in insomnia.

We know that our stress response consists of a series of hormonal messages, but it is the prolonged activation of these that can have a knock-on impact on the function of other *hormonal processes* in our body. Stress can influence many other hormonal conditions such as menstrual and fertility issues, menopausal symptoms, and auto-immune conditions such as hypothyroidism, and can also influence conditions such as diabetes due to the influence that stress has on blood sugar levels.

Very often, we may be completely unaware of how stress and our Worry Warrior are impacting our body, although one very common feature we may notice if we feel stress, is tension in our muscles. If ongoing, this tension can lead to long-term muscle and joint problems as the tension interrupts normal movement. In addition to this, any pain can also be intensified in stress mode as our nervous system becomes more sensitised, turning up the volume of the pain.

We often assume that the degree of pain we feel, must equate to a similar degree of trauma to our tissue, i.e., intense pain equals severe trauma, however, this is not always the case.

When the Worry Warrior mode is active, intense pain can be felt that far outweighs the degree of any trauma. In fact, the Worry Warrior's presence may be accompanied by ongoing persistent pain that has no physical origin at all. This pain is still every bit as real as that caused by physical trauma. When the stress response is more active the brain interprets pain messages as more significant and therefore will increase the intensity of the pain perception.

To make matters worse, clients may find their stress levels rising because the usual physical investigations may find no apparent cause for the debilitating pain that they feel. Therefore, recognising that emotional distress can cause physical pain is an important factor in finding a way to put this kind of persistent pain in the past.

I have helped many people, particularly with *back pain and sciatica* who have tried many different treatments but had previously found no relief; some have even had surgery to address the pain, yet still were limited by persistent pain. However, the common theme of stress had not been explored, with their emotional wellbeing not having been previously included in their treatment plan.

By investing time in addressing this area together we found a solution that brought changes way beyond their expectations, not only finding freedom from pain but also feeling that they could live their life in a more calm, contented and relaxed way.

Migraines are another common problem that may have stress at the heart of the presentation. Migraines that give rise to several debilitating symptoms, can often demonstrate the physical presentation of an ongoing stress reaction.

Increased nerve sensitivity, blood vessel and muscle tension, and digestive system disturbances, can all contribute to symptoms of intense pain such as visual disturbances, motion sensitivity, photophobia, nausea and vomiting, so commonly seen in migraines.

Great success can therefore be achieved by addressing the factors that are triggering the stress response in the treatment of migraines.

Because the stress response is an unconscious reaction, we may not make the connection between how we feel physically with how we feel emotionally. If we are so used to living life in Worry Warrior mode, we may not even recognise that we are living in an active stress response.

I have worked with clients who wouldn't classify themselves as being stressed but, when we discuss how they feel the majority of the time, it becomes apparent that their Worry Warrior is getting in their way; they just had never lived life any differently to realise.

It was so refreshing to hear a client of mine recently say, "If ever I notice new aches or pain now, I firstly ask myself, what's going on around me at the moment? I recognise that feeling more stressed can impact how I feel physically."

Once we recognise the signs that our Worry Warrior is active then we have made the first step to making a change.

Understanding this connection makes complete sense of why we may have been struggling in the past and it also means the future can feel very different too.

This puts us in a much stronger position, giving us so much more choice about how we live our lives, rather than continuing the cycle of letting life happen to us.

Chapter Four

Making Change Happen The APPEAR Process

So far, we have explored the science behind stress and the negative impacts it can have on us.

Once you have decided that there could be many benefits from letting go of your Worry Warrior you are probably keen to understand how you could do that!

So, in the rest of the book, I'm going to share with you a simple six-step process that I have created called the APPEAR process, this will help you begin to understand your Worry Warrior and discover how you can bring about change to calm it.

This process will show you how you can rewrite your story, discover who you really are, create the life you want to lead and also find more peace, happiness and contentment in all that you do.

Here are the six steps that we will be looking at in more detail over the next few chapters:

A=**Aware** In this section you will become more aware of what triggers your Worry Warrior into action. It will help you understand more about yourself, who you really are, and what's getting in the way of you making the changes you want to make. It will help you become clearer about your priorities and identify whether or not you are living your life in alignment with them.

P=**Purpose** Looking at Purpose you will explore the benefits of making change and explore how life will be once you have made that change, setting out your intention for the future. Being clear about your Purpose is so important, this will be the drive for change and will guide you towards your future goals.

P=**Perception** Here you will begin to understand how changing your perception of situations can completely change how you feel about them and this in turn can result in calming your Worry Warrior. You will learn that you can rewrite programmes that have been getting in your way to create more helpful automatic responses, giving you the choice to think, feel and act how you would like to.

E=**Emotional Intention** In this section you will understand the importance of how your mindset and emotional state will influence the outcome of any situation. It will show you how to set clear intentions for how you will be feeling in the future, resulting in a more positive approach to life and allowing you to reach the outcomes you desire so much more easily.

A=**Actions** Action must always accompany intention in order to achieve change, so this section focuses on what actions will support the change you want to make. It will give you ideas and structure to take positive action towards the life you want to lead.

R=**Resources**. Here you will look at the different types of support and tools that might help you make the changes you are aiming for.

We will bring together all of the exercises in this book giving you a checklist to follow so that you can collate your reflections and create your Mind Fit Map; your personal guide to Calm your Worry Warrior.

Chapter Five

AWARE What's Triggering Your Worry Warrior?

The first step in making any change to our Worry Warrior is to become aware of its presence and then recognise the impact that it has on us.

As we know, our Worry Warrior may present itself with uncomfortable feelings, unhelpful behaviours or perhaps even changes to our physical body.

Sometimes we may immediately recognise the source of feeling stressed and seek help to address these difficulties, which makes the process of addressing our Worry Warriors so much easier.

However, on occasions, we may recognise the difficulties our Worry Warrior brings but we don't seem to see any reason for it. This can mean we feel even more stressed; we can't find the reason for feeling the way we do so that makes us feel even worse.

We may be thinking 'If I can't find a reason, how can I fix it?'

There may also be times when our Worry Warrior does such a good job of covering up the difficulties, that we may not even recognise that stress or our Worry Warrior are the actual problem.

In these circumstances, we may develop coping strategies, such as overworking, over-exercising, over and under-eating or excessive drinking to create a numbing effect for us, hiding what's really going on below the surface. These actions work to suppress any uncomfortable emotions - we learn that these activities give us a positive boost or a short-term hit, but in the long term, they can be detrimental to our wellbeing.

We may try to address the fallout from these actions; for example, dealing with injuries from overtraining, dieting to lose weight or changing jobs to reduce the feelings of burnout; but it's not until we recognise that it is our Worry Warrior that is triggering these behaviours that we will find long-term solutions to these difficulties.

Spending time exploring what might be triggering unhelpful feelings, emotions or behaviours is the first place to start. Very often there may be many things that together are filling up our Stress Bucket and result in our Worry Warrior Mode being active.

Becoming more self-aware, and finding what's behind our thoughts, our actions and our emotions is something that can take time to perfect but, when we spend time putting attention into this area, we will see the results. We can then discover the difference between our Worry Warrior responses and our true self; that's the first step to making a change.

In earlier chapters we reviewed that often, it's not a situation itself that triggers our Worry Warrior into action, it is more about our beliefs and expectations connected to that situation that will trigger its presence.

Taking a look into our beliefs and expectations can be the key to unlocking unhelpful patterns. Once we identify the expectation that can be triggering the response itself, we will know what we need to work on to get a different outcome.

There are very often common themes present that can be triggers for our Worry Warrior to take over, sometimes finding that below the surface, fear is at the root of things.

Looking at some examples of clients' stories will highlight some of the themes that frequently arise and will demonstrate how becoming AWARE will begin the journey to Calm our Worry Warrior.

Mary's Story

Mary came to see me as she was feeling so overwhelmed with all the things she needed to do. She had a busy job and a teenage family. She felt her job was causing her the most stress in her life, but she began to recognise that it was her feelings about the responsibility of all she needed to do that was causing her to feel overwhelmed.

She began to understand that the *need to please others* was always such a high priority for her, that often she put her own needs at the bottom of the list; behind her overwhelm she discovered, was the fear of being rejected.

This need to please led Mary to feel that she was always carrying the burden of meeting everyone else's needs; this felt like a huge responsibility that she struggled to meet. Mary recognised that this was one of the beliefs that was triggering her Worry Warrior to be present.

However, on deeper reflection, she realised that this wasn't true. It wasn't her responsibility to meet every single need of those around her. Her awareness and recognition of this was the first step to change that unhelpful expectation of rejection and to free herself from the pressure and burden that brought.

Jackie's Story

When working with Jackie, she suggested that one of the reasons that she was feeling stressed was due to the demands that were arising from managing her mum's care; but, as this was something that she wanted to provide herself, she needed to find a way to deal with it.

What Jackie didn't realise, until we worked together, was that there were emotions hidden below the surface. Jackie discovered that being with her mum triggered old uncomfortable feelings. Feelings of *not being good enough*, and questioning herself, did she meet her mum's expectations?

Jackie realised that these feelings and beliefs were something that she had formed when she was a young child, and they weren't at all relevant today.

She realised that even though this was an old programme, it was still causing her Worry Warrior to be present and this was getting in the way of doing what she wanted currently. This awareness made it so much easier for her to look forward and see a way to change the situation.

Tracey's Story

Tracey's story shows how *uncertainty* can be one of the triggers for feeling uncomfortable and stressed. This is a common theme that triggers the stress response within us. When Tracey came to me, she was dealing with the fact that her husband had been admitted to hospital and there was no clarity around how his illness was going to be managed. Besides the obvious concerns that accompany a loved one being unwell, Tracey was feeling extremely anxious, noticing an inner feeling of overwhelm all the time.

This anxiety was having a physical impact on her body too; ongoing back pain that she had experienced for many years had flared up. At the time, she wasn't aware that the pain was connected to her emotional state but, when I explained that her current stress could impact her physical body, it made perfect sense to her that the two were connected.

We went on to uncover other unhelpful beliefs and exceptions that were contributing to her difficulties, and these were all adding together to bring a feeling of total overwhelm. Highlighting these issues was the start of change for Tracey and working from here, we were able to help her reduce her pain levels and bring her to a much calmer and happier place.

Ann's Story

Ann was another client who asked me for help due to feeling overwhelmed. She wanted to get past the procrastination cycle she was in as it was stopping her from developing her business. Ann was desperate to 'get things done' and the less this happened, the more she experienced a constant feeling of overwhelm.

When exploring what was behind her procrastination, we discovered it was simply a *fear of getting things wrong*.

Ann mentioned that the thought of getting something wrong made her feel so vulnerable she was afraid to decide on doing anything.

As a result, Ann's Worry Warrior had jumped into action; her unconscious processing was driving her in a direction to avoid getting things wrong, resulting in her not taking action on her new business initiatives.

Again, this may have arisen from patterns learnt as a child, connected to a difficult experience from that time.

Unhelpful programmes can, however, be set up at any point in time in our lives, the significant factor being the severity of the uncomfortable emotion that is created at the time of that situation occurring.

As Ann became aware of her fear, she was then in a position to work on that fear to bring about more confidence and improved focus with her business ventures.

Grief and traumatic events may be other factors that can add to an increase in our stress levels on an ongoing basis.

We may re-experience the emotions connected to a past event with the same intensity as if it were happening right now.

Loss of a loved one is always going to be a sad experience but, in some cases, the intensity of that loss and the emotions connected to it can continue long after the event of the actual loss.

The pain of loss can be sitting below the surface, and it can take a great deal of unconscious effort to keep it under wraps. Not being able to process this emotion properly can be a major factor in increasing stress levels.

Susan's Story

For Susan, becoming aware of the need to deal with the emotions connected to the loss of her mother was a starting place for her programme.

Although aware of how uncomfortable the loss was, she had been unaware of the significance this was having on the depression, anxiety and physical pain she was experiencing. What a relief it was for her to discover that there was a way to move forward from it in a more positive way.

Linda's Story

Linda was another client who recognised that she was a long-term worrier but hadn't realised that a traumatic event that occurred twenty years previously was still having an impact on her in the present.

Linda had come to me for physiotherapy to help with her neck pain, but during the assessment, she also mentioned the struggles she had with ongoing migraines. These could result in her being confined to bed for 24 hours, plus additional days following this for her to recover to full function again.

Numerous investigations and consultant opinions reassured her there was no serious pathology causing the headaches, so Linda had assumed that the Migraines would just be part of her life. I explained to Linda that they could be arising because her Worry Warrior was so often present, and we began to explore the reasons for this.

High on the list of things that have been difficult for Linda to deal with was the time her son became unwell, twenty years ago. Aged four, he had been taken suddenly ill and had required life-saving surgery. Thankfully, her son recovered but is still dealing with the aftereffects of the surgery, along with the possibility that he may, at some point in the future, need further life-saving surgery.

Linda had assumed the ongoing difficulties of the stress she was experiencing had more to do with the current challenges she faced, but she discovered that the trigger for the most uncomfortable feelings was indeed associated with the memory of the initial event of her son's illness.

These feelings were frequently being triggered when she was dealing with her son, reliving the fear she felt at the time and so we addressed this as a priority. We are often completely unaware of the impact that difficult situations from the past can have on our current situation.

I have helped clients deal with all sorts of trauma from the past. Some may be quite horrific events such as sexual abuse, domestic violence or catastrophic illness; but other events may appear to be of less significance, such as bullying, the end of a relationship, or failure to succeed. These seemingly less significant events can still create intense distress and consequently can have a similarly severe impact on us, switching our Worry Warrior mode on constantly.

We cannot judge the impact that any of these events will have on a particular individual - we all respond to situations in different ways.

If a situation was hugely distressing for the individual at the time, and they have not been able to process that distress, then it can continue to reproduce intensely difficult emotions in the present, in all sorts of ways.

Having looked at these different scenarios, we can see how becoming aware of what's behind our Worry Warrior is the first step to making a change. Asking ourselves, Is my Worry Warrior taking over? Why does it feel the need to protect me? What is the fear behind it?

There is a common thread to all of these stories that trigger our Worry Warrior and that is the perception of vulnerability. I wouldn't be surprised if the stories I have shared perhaps strike a chord with you, or perhaps you know someone who might present with a similar story.

Most of us at some point will have experienced situations where we feel vulnerable; it's part of being human. Facing vulnerabilities can be a difficult thing but, when we do, we can often find hugely rewarding and liberating results.

Our fears and negative beliefs hold us back from being who we really are; it's important to remember that these beliefs don't arise from *who* we are but instead are the result of our interpretation of the experiences we have had.

It can be quite reassuring to recognise that, "It's not me, it's my Worry Worrier that is creating this reaction!"

Some of us mistakenly believe that it's safer to keep our vulnerabilities under wraps but it's only when we face them that we can address and be free of them.

By becoming AWARE of our inner fears, negative beliefs and expectations, we are empowering ourselves to begin the journey of discovering the person we are truly meant to be.

"Owning our story can be hard, but not nearly as difficult as spending our lives running from it....."

"Imperfections are not inadequacies; they are reminders that we're all in this together." Brené Brown

Helping You Become More AWARE of What is Behind Your Worry Warrior's Presence

We have looked at some examples of how unhelpful programming has got in the way of others, so the next step is to help you become more aware of what's getting in *your* way.

As you've decided to read this book, I assume that you are already connecting with the idea that your Worry Warrior may be responsible for some of the difficulties that you are currently facing but, if you're not entirely sure, then have a look at this quiz below.

Worry Warrior Quiz

Have a look at this list, and see how many of the following questions apply to you:

1. I often feel anxious and find I am often worrying about what has happened or might happen in the future.
2. I question my decisions, always asking myself, am I doing the right thing?
3. I find it difficult to get myself out of a low mood.

4. I am often worried about what other people think of me.
5. I find myself getting angry and find it difficult to control this.
6. I feel overwhelmed with all that I need to do.
7. I place other people's needs above my own.
8. I feel stuck and don't know how to change the situation.
9. I find myself acting in a way I later regret.
10. I find that there are often things I would love to do but somehow, I can't.
11. I find it hard to relax, my brain never wants to switch off.
12. I have ongoing pain that restricts what I can do on occasions.
13. I have some allergies or sensitivities.
14. I frequently suffer from migraines.
15. I have been diagnosed with an autoimmune problem.
16. I have to be careful what I eat as I am prone to irritable bowel symptoms.

How many of these did you tick? If you agreed with *any* of these statements it could mean that your Worry Warrior is getting in your way of living life to the full. The more you have ticked, the more likely it is that Calming your Worry Warrior will have a positive impact on your life.

Focusing our AWARENESS

We have already mentioned that the more our Stress Bucket is filled with unhelpful beliefs and difficult past experiences, the more likely our Worry Warrior will be active.

Next, we will explore the key areas of your life that could be contributing to filling up the Stress Bucket. The Wheel of Life exercise will help you flag up the areas that feel most challenging for you and will also highlight those that are working well for you too.

This will give you some focus on where change may be helpful and will help clarify where to begin to put your attention to make that change.

Wheel of Life Exercise

The Wheel Life exercise is designed to take a broad look across all areas of our life so that we can reflect on what's good and what feels like there is room for improvement too.

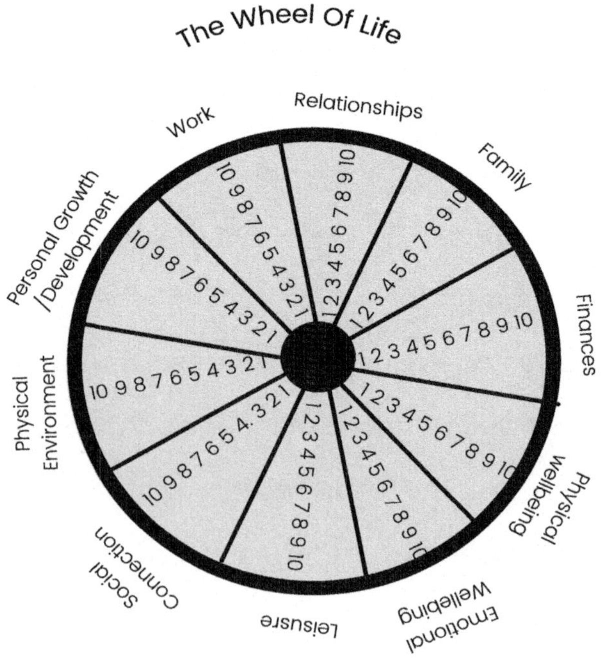

In this exercise, we score how active our Worry Warrior is in each area and then spend some time reflecting on why we have given it that score. This helps us become more AWARE of the areas we need to focus on in the first instance.

On the wheel, which is divided up into sections, we score each section from 1 to 10, with 1 being where we feel most stressed or anxious, (with our Worry Warrior being most active) and 10 being the happiest score, when everything feels content and as it should be.

What we are aiming for is balance across the whole wheel, if particular areas are much lower in score than others then these are the areas to focus on initially.

For any area that scored lower than a 6, consider the challenges that are present in this area and then reflect on the reasons this score has been given.

Following on from this, we can then consider if any unhelpful beliefs may be connected to this. This reflection helps us to gradually uncover what is behind the difficulties in this area.

It's also important to reflect on what is good and working well in our life; it's all too easy to only focus on what's not good when our Worry Warrior is active so it's a good habit to put some attention into any successes in our life as well. This helps begin to restore the balance that we are looking for.

For the areas of the Wheel where the score is higher than a 6, spend some time reflecting on why it does feel good. What's going well here? And what are the beliefs attached to this?

If there are no scores above 6 in any sections, that's okay too. This gives us an understanding that there is some work to do across the board. The good thing is, we have now made the choice; it's time to make some changes and we are committed to finding out how to do that.

If it feels a bit uncomfortable looking at the lists of negative things showing up in our lives, we should try to see what we have uncovered as a positive. Remember this is only a reflection of where we are today; not where we want to be.

Exposing our vulnerabilities can be ultimately empowering, it is the first step to making change.

Completing this exercise shows the intent to change and that is one of the most powerful ingredients in making a positive difference.

Here is an example of the scores and the unhelpful beliefs that Mary uncovered in her Wheel of Life exercise.

Area in Wheel of Life	Score 1-10	Reasons for Score *Why does this feel good? /What is the challenge? What is/ isn't working well?*	Beliefs and expectations *What am I afraid might happen?*
Work A job that meets your purpose	5	I spend a lot of time feeling as if haven't got enough time to get everything done. I panic if I have to present work to others and if I am put on the spot to answer questions.	I might let others down. My work might not be good enough. What will others think of me? My mind always goes blank when I stand up to talk.
Relationship A relationship that meets your individual needs	6	I have a loving and supportive partner; I wish I could enjoy our time together more as I am spending too much time with worrying thoughts in my head.	I often have a feeling that things might go wrong so when we plan anything nice, I worry about all the things that could go wrong and find I'm thinking about that, rather than enjoying what we are doing.
Family Balance within your family relationships	5	Family life can be difficult sometimes, it feels like I am juggling so many balls, there is so much to do. I feel as if everyone else is enjoying life, but I never seem to get done what I want for myself.	I am worried that everyone won't have what they need. I don't want to see anyone upset and feel I need to be one step ahead of everyone so that I can anticipate their needs.
Finances Feeling confident and secure around your money	6	Money is ok but there is always a constant pressure to earn a bit more and I am always thinking of ways to make that happen.	I always worry that there won't be enough money coming in for what we need. I am always a little afraid when we make a new financial commitment.
Physical Wellbeing Feeling fit and healthy	8	I am fit and well and make an effort to look after my health.	It's important to eat well and exercise and I enjoy feeling that my body works well for me.
Emotional Wellbeing Feeling happy and content	4	I often feel overwhelmed and stressed out and wish I could enjoy the moment a bit more.	I'm never going to feel calm and content when I have all I have to do. I can't see how to change things.
Leisure Fun without purpose	4	I don't have any hobbies or spend time doing things just for fun.	I don't have the time for any hobbies.
Social Connection Sharing Friendships	7	I have some great friends though I do worry about going out and meeting new people.	"What will people think of me?" is the top of my worries if I meet someone new.
Physical Environment Living and working conditions	7	I have a nice home though we would like to move at some point in the future. I would like to live somewhere more rural.	What might happen if we move somewhere new, what if we don't like it?
Personal Growth/ Development Feeding your soul	5	I do training at work that is requested by my company but don't do much just for me. There are several things I would like to try, but never give them a priority.	There is never much time for me to give this much thought.

You can use the Wheel of Life activity sheet in Chapter Eleven *'Creating Your MindFit Map'* section to carry out this exercise yourself.

Once you have spent some time working through your Wheel of Life exercise, were there any surprises for you?

Has it helped you to understand where to put your attention in the first instance?

Has it helped you understand which areas of your life are the biggest triggers for Your Worry Warrior to be jumping into action?

Are you a little clearer about what unhelpful beliefs and expectations could be getting in your way?

Moving on from there, it can also be helpful for you to consider if there are any other situations where you see your Worry Warrior showing up, that we haven't included in the Wheel of Life.

As mentioned before, the memory of traumatic events in our past or difficult situations we have experienced can leave us with uncomfortable programmes that keep replaying themselves, triggering our Worry Warrior's reaction.

Are there any old difficult experiences which could be triggering difficult reactions for you; could they be stopping you from moving forward in a positive way?

If there are, make a list of them; describe the situation, and then think about whether you have any unhelpful beliefs or expectations that arise from these situations, just as you did in the Wheel of Life.

It is important to be aware of the impact these situations may be having on your life today but remember it is possible to change that too.

Now you have begun to explore what could be filling up your Stress Bucket and what may be triggering your Worry Warrior into action. That's the first step of the process, in the next chapter, we will look at the next step in the APPEAR process, finding your PURPOSE for change.

Chapter Six

PURPOSE For Change

Now that we have identified what needs to change, it's time for the next step in the APPEAR Process - PURPOSE for change.

Our brain is primarily driven by two main functions - to take us away from danger and also to take us towards pleasure.

If we are in Worry Warrior mode, our focus will often be on moving away from the negatives and this may well result in us ending up somewhere we don't want to be.

We can begin to train our brains towards a more positive focus; the place where we do want to be and therefore having more chance of getting there.

Having this positive purpose and direction will make it much easier for our brain to accept change and as a result, our Worry Warrior will be much less likely to be present.

To identify our PURPOSE, we might like to consider several questions:

- What is the PURPOSE for you to make that change?
- What direction do you want to be heading?
- Why is this change so important for you?
- How will life be once you have let go of your Worry Warrior?
- What good things will come from making these changes?
- What will it mean for you?
- What are the benefits of making a change?
- What will be better?
- What will be easier?

Consider these questions, reflect on them and use the answers to help you recognise the benefits of making a change.

Values

It's important when formulating your PURPOSE for change that you keep in mind what is important to you as a person. We need to be mindful that the PURPOSE for change is consistent with our values and priorities in life.

The next exercise will give you the chance to discover what your values are and will allow you the time to reflect on whether those values are currently showing up as a priority in your life.

We may not have given this any consideration at all in the past, perhaps finding that we have allowed life to happen to us, rather than focusing on what is important to us and how we want life to be.

If we are not living life in alignment with our values, then we are more likely to feel stress. Highlighting our values and ensuring our PURPOSE is aligned with them will improve the likelihood of reaching our goals.

Living by Our Values Exercise

(You will find a template of *Living by your Values Action Sheet* in Chapter Eleven, *Creating Your MindFit Map.)*

The following exercise will bring more clarity and focus to your values and the things that are currently important to you in your life at the moment.

On the list over the page, highlight each word that resonates with you. Don't think about it too much, just go with your first gut reaction to each word.

- Then go through the words you have marked and pick out five of these words that feel most important to you.
- Write these five words (in order) in the CORE section below.
- Then return to the original list of those you highlighted and write the next five most important words into the GROWTH section below.
- Repeat with the next five most important words and write them in the FLOURISH Section.

Values:

*Acceptance *Control *Humour

*Privacy *Success

*Achievement *Creativity * Imagination *Productivity

*Teaching *Adventure

*Equality *Independence *Promotion

*Prospects *Teamwork * Altruism *Status

*Excellence *Influence *Reaching potential

*Tolerance * Ambition * Excitement *Intellect

*Recognition *Tradition *Appreciation

*Expertise

*Intuition *Respect *Travel *Authenticity

*Fairness *Justice *Responsibility *Trust

*Authority

*Faith *Kindness * Results * Variety *Autonomy

*Fame *Leadership *Risk taking *Winning

*Balance *Family * Learning * Romance

*Wisdom

*Beauty *Fast pace * Love *Routine

*Zest for life *Belonging *Financial rewards

*Loyalty *Safety *Certainty *Focus

*Making a difference

*Security * Challenge *Freedom

*Nurturing *Self Expression *Collaboration *Fun *Order

*Service

*Commitment *Happiness *Passion *Sharing

*Compassion *Health * Perfection *Spirituality *Connection

*Helping Others *Personal Growth

*Stability *Contribution *Honesty *Power

CORE:	GROWTH:	FLOURISH:
1	1	1
2	2	2
3	3	3
4	4	4
5	5	5

The CORE values are the most fundamental to our basic happiness.

The GROWTH values will further support your enjoyment in life.

The FLOURISH values bring a higher fulfilment to your life.

Once you have completed the exercise spend some time reflecting on your lists.

- How much attention do you put into these values in your life?
- Does it feel as if these values are fulfilled in your life?
- Does it feel as if these values support the direction you want to be moving towards?

Each of us will have our own individual set of values personal to us and they may well change over time. As we move through life our focus and responsibilities may change. This is why it's important to review our values regularly as our life and roles within them may change.

For example, the values and focus we have as a twenty-year-old student may well be very different from a forty-year-old businesswoman When we transition from one phase in our life to another, reviewing our values and ensuring that we live according to those, means we are living life, true to who we really are.

Making life choices that are true to yourself is a sure way to help keep your Worry Warrior in check and live a more fulfilling life.

Ann's Values

Ann found that one of the values in her Flourish list was Adventure. She reported that adventure was the 'icing on the cake' in her life. On further discussion, she recognised that this need was only met by her annual two-week holiday. She realised that she spent all year looking forward to that adventure, but only actually experienced adventure for two weeks each year of her life.

As wonderful as the holidays were, she wanted to continue with this theme of adventure on a more regular basis, so she decided to include more adventure every week.

This might only be small events, such as choosing a different place to explore on a walk, but it meant that this Flourish value was met for her regularly.

Jackie's Values

When we discussed with Jackie what she wanted for the future, one of the things she wanted was to be able to lose weight. Jackie felt that she had been overweight for many years and was unhappy with how she felt.

When she looked at her values, her list showed Family high on the list of importance along with Kindness and Making a Difference; this was all in line with her desire to support her mum's additional care needs.

However, Jackie noticed that there was nothing there that would support her goal of losing weight. She realised she hadn't included health as a priority even though this was one of her main drivers to lose weight.

As a result, it made sense to Jackie that achieving her wellbeing goals would continue to be a struggle until she put some focus into this area.

Jackie realised that it was time for her to include this in her purpose, time for her to pay attention to her wellbeing as well as those she was helping.

This is a good example of how we can be living our lives with out-of-date values which can leave us feeling frustrated and stressed, another reason our Worry Warrior can't settle.

Tracey's Values

Tracey included Security on her list, the need to feel safe was very important to her. It meant that she made choices that would increase the feeling of safety for her.

What she hadn't realised though, was that this could mean that fundamentally she had a fear that she wasn't safe, always striving to achieve that feeling of safety in all she did.

For Tracey, carrying out this exercise flagged up an unhelpful belief, something we could work with to help her feel more confident in the future.

This shows us how looking at our values can reveal things that are holding us back as well as things that can improve our life.

Having completed the Values exercise we have more information that will help shape our PURPOSE for change, enabling us to clarify where we want to be and why.

By being clear about our PURPOSE for change, we are also defining our markers for success. Just like entering the correct address in the satnav, if you don't know where you are going, you won't know when you get there!

Success will be different for each of us; what's very important is that you identify what success means *for you*, your definition, based on you as a person, on your values and circumstances in your life.

And remember, those definitions can change throughout our life so, again, review your definition of PURPOSE and success at regular intervals in your life. Keep your PURPOSE up to date to ensure that your life feels fulfilled and contented.

When we are looking at how our life will be in the future, it's important to focus on what you *do* want, rather than what you don't.

Based on the rule, **We Find What We Focus On**, it is very important to see our vision from the positive rather than the negative perspective.

If we focus on, 'I don't want to feel overwhelmed at work,' then our brain focuses on 'the overwhelm' and it will be difficult to direct it anywhere else.

However, if our plan is, 'To have a job that I enjoy and feel I make a difference every day' it's a much easier task to achieve, remember the satnav; choose your destination wisely!

Clarifying your PURPOSE gives you motivation, focus and direction, and will help persuade your Worry Warrior that its input isn't required.

Of course, there is more to it than just positive thinking, but this positive focus is important in creating your goal.

In the past we may not even have considered how good things might be in the future, all we have been able to focus on is not wanting to be or feel like we do right now.

So, the next step for you to take is to identify the different elements of your PURPOSE for change.

Create a list of what you want to achieve, starting with the areas you flagged up in the Wheel of Life and identify what will be different for you in the future once you have calmed your Worry Warrior.

Consider the questions we reviewed earlier and include what you discovered in your Living by Your Values Exercise.

You can record your thoughts in the PURPOSE for Change template which you can find in Chapter Eleven, *Creating your MindFit Map*. Feel free to add more to your list than space allows or feel comfortable setting just one goal too. Remember this process is individual so each of us should do what feels right for us at this time.

Having completed your PURPOSE for Change Exercise hopefully, the real benefits of Calming your Worry Warrior have become clearer, and you are ready for the next exciting step, changing your PERCEPTION of the situation to create your new reality.

Area of Wheel of Life	PURPOSE for change What will the change mean for you? What are you now able to do?
Work *A job that meets your purpose.*	I am enjoying work and feel I have enough time to get done all that is needed. I am confident to present my work and ideas to others.
Relationship *A relationship that meets your individual needs.*	I am excited about events that we plan and feel so much more in the present when we are doing them.
Family *Balance within your family relationships.*	I am confident with my decisions and appreciate that other's opinions may be different from mine. I am comfortable visiting my parents and enjoy their company.
Finances *Feeling confident and secure around your money.*	I feel secure financially and I have a clear plan for my finances in the future.
Physical Wellbeing *Feeling fit and healthy.*	I continue to enjoy good health and stay fit and active.
Emotional Wellbeing *Feeling happy and content.*	I feel calm confident and contented with where I am in my life.
Leisure *Fun without purpose.*	I find time to read my book now and I incorporate fun activities into my fitness regime such as trampolining and cycling with the children.
Social connection *Sharing Friendships*	I am more confident meeting new people, so it's easier for me to enjoy time going out and attending things like parties.
Physical Environment *Living and working conditions*	It feels more realistic to consider moving to a more rural location where the whole family can enjoy the benefits of the outdoors more.
Personal Growth/Development *Feeding your Soul*	I recognise my strengths and now feel more confident to consider taking on more responsibility at work. I am also exploring the possibility now of training to be a netball coach to support my daughter's team.

Here is the example of Mary's PURPOSE for change exercise which she drew up after her Wheel of Life Review

Chapter Seven

PERCEPTION Creating Your Reality

We all see the world from a different place because we have all experienced different things and therefore have created different versions of reality along the way.

That's why we may have different opinions about things in life and why we can all make different choices in life too; we will see life from different perspectives. This explains why some of us may find some situations challenging and fearful and others do not.

Very often I hear people who experience anxiety, expressing their frustration that they know a situation shouldn't feel difficult or uncomfortable and they wish they could control how they feel.

Not only can there be a difference between each of us, as individuals, but we can also find a difference between our rational conscious self and our unconscious self (our automatic programming). We see the situation in one way, but our brain has been programmed to respond in another.

The brain perceives the situation to be a threat, and perhaps, at some point in our life that situation did pose a threat to us, but now in the present day, if able to rationalise it, it would seem much less of a challenge.

This is when our Worry Warrior jumps into action before we get a chance to choose how we might like to respond because those old programmes repeat the same old response.

Being able to look at things from a different perspective can mean that we can react differently. If our PERCEPTION of the situation changes then our reaction can be different too.

That is why our next step in the APPEAR process is to change our PERCEPTION.

Take a look at the picture on the next page and see if you can find the two different women in the picture. Depending on how you see this picture will change how you perceive the woman that is in it.

Did you first see an old lady with a pointy nose and a shawl wrapped around her head or did you see the young lady in side profile with a choker necklace around her neck and a big black hat?

Both ways of seeing the picture are a truth of a kind, neither is right nor wrong, just different.

But, if we put our attention on one or other of the images, and keep our focus on that, eventually when we look at that picture, we will only see the picture that we have chosen to see.

What we are doing here is choosing the reality we wish to see, so changing our PERCEPTION and our reaction to it.

To help convince your Worry Warrior that it is time to change its PERCEPTION, we can start to explore what is our version of the truth that we want to see.

Testing the Evidence to Uncover the Truth.

When looking at unhelpful beliefs and expectations we can question their validity by asking ourselves the following questions:

- Is that belief the case today?
- Where is the evidence to support that expectation?
- When was that belief created?
- Is that belief relevant to me today?

We are then likely to recognise the unhelpful belief is no longer, or maybe never was, relevant to us. Perhaps it was a belief owned by someone significant to us that we adopted along the way, but now we can see it is something we would rather let go of. *We can then decide what would be an alternative way to view a situation by asking ourselves:*

- Is there a more helpful way to see this?
- How would I prefer to think/feel/act?
- What will be the purpose of changing this belief? (if you're following the APPEAR process you will already have clarified this in your PURPOSE for Change)

It is these questions that will help us form a new perspective on the situation, changing our PERCEPTION, and creating our new truth.

After this, we can move towards accepting this new truth and making it part of our automatic programming.

You can use the PERCEPTION Action sheet to help you re-assess unhelpful beliefs and expectations. (Find the template in Chapter Eleven *Creating Your MindFit Map).*

Here is an example of the notes Mary made when looking at how she could change her perception:

Area of Wheel of Life	Look at any unhelpful fears or beliefs and see how you can see things differently. What evidence is there that proves a different perspective? How can you see it differently?
Work	I always reach my deadlines, so I know that I have sufficient time to get everything done. My boss often praises the work I do.
Relationship	We always have a good time when we are together. I know that things generally do go according to plan when we are arranging events and if any problems arise, I am very capable of resolving them.
Family	Each of us is responsible for our happiness. I can support my family members in finding happiness, but it isn't solely my responsibility. Others can support me too.
Finances	We always have enough money to do what we need to and are always able to find the money we need for things we like to do.
Physical Wellbeing	I continue to enjoy good health and stay fit and active.
Emotional Wellbeing	I understand that I feel the way I do because of old unhelpful programmes that keep getting in my way and I now understand that it is possible to change that.
Leisure	Prioritising time for myself is important so that I can refresh and recharge and it's ok for me to do that
Social connection	I recognise that other people's judgment of me is a reflection of who they are rather than a truth about me. If I am happy with who I am that is what is important.
Physical	If we decide to move, we will have given it due consideration

Environment	from all angles so we will be confident with our choice.
Personal Growth/ Development	I recognise that I am hard working and learn things quickly and have a lot to offer the company I work for. I can now look at how I could progress in my role in the future.

Changing our Perception for Good

To change our perception for good we need to create new, more helpful programmes in our brain that support a different perspective.

If we understand the key concepts that relate to the development of such programmes, we are in a much better place to influence their creation.

I have identified five key areas that should be considered when looking at developing new and lasting neural programmes which can influence how we think, feel and behave.

To help remember them I have chosen the word ARISE as a prompt, each letter representing a key area to be considered.

Attention

Repetition

Imagination

Significance

Emotions

Attention

The first principle of re-programming a new PERCEPTION is to be clear about where you are putting your ATTENTION.

You have already become AWARE of what you would like to change and perhaps you have discovered that there are a number of things filing up your Stress Bucket.

So, the next thing to decide is, what is the most relevant or important area of change for you? Don't try to make too many changes at once, remember one step at a time, and each little step will be taking you one step closer to your destination. That way you will gradually empty your Stress Bucket, turn down your stress response, and bring your Worry Warrior to rest.

We Find What We Focus On, so be clear about where you place your attention so that you get the results you desire.

We must be sure to place our ATTENTION on the positive; what we *do* want to achieve, how we *do* want to feel, where we *do* want to be, rather than what we don't want.

If we think, 'I don't want to feel stressed/angry/upset, etc', this still keeps our attention on what we don't want.

A more helpful focus of attention would therefore be, 'I am calm/happy/content, etc.'

This will guide your unconscious in the direction you want to be, even if at this point you may not feel that is the case. This prepares your brain for that situation, just like a rehearsal.

Repetition

Practice Makes Permanent

The more we repeat a programme the more it will show up again; it makes no difference whether that programme is beneficial to us or not, the more it is repeated the stronger it gets.

Therefore, it stands to reason that the more we practise where we want to be, the more likely we are to get there.

We are all probably familiar with the process of repetition when learning something new.

Perhaps you have learnt to drive and can remember how initially, you had to consciously think about every element of the process, 'mirror, signal, manoeuvre'.

But, after a lot of practise, and repeating the same process, you became completely competent with all the skills needed to drive, carrying out all the necessary procedures automatically.

REPETITION and regular practise of what you want and where you want to be is a vital component of creating that new programme.

This will open up new neural pathways in the brain; It's like treading a new path through a field, the more times you walk it the more defined it becomes.

Imagination

Now it may seem a challenge to practise how we want things to be if your Worry Warrior is jumping into play every time we are in a trigger situation.

This is where we can use a very powerful tool that can be carried around with us always … our imagination.

We can use our imagination to create a different image in our mind of how we want things to be. We can practise this in an environment that feels safe and comfortable, away from the trigger events.

Our brain does not differentiate between what is real and what is imagined. This is why unhelpful reactions can often be triggered just by thinking about a difficult situation. The same neural pathways will be active in our brain whether we are actually doing something or whether we were just imagining that we're doing it.

Within many sports, visualisation is frequently used to perfect technique.

You may have seen a professional sports player pause before they take a penalty kick, for example, where they run through every detail in their head before actually taking action.

They will have spent many hours practising this mental rehearsal to perfect the action needed in their game; creating permanent neural pathways that they will tap into with the visualisation, just before the real event.

There are numerous studies that have shown that the results from mental rehearsal can prove more successful than actual physical practices, because each time you imagine the exact technique, you are creating the perfect neural pathway.

However, when we physically practise something, there is likely to be an error in the activity until our muscles have learned the correct sequence, so it can take a lot longer to perfect from physical practice alone.

The use of our imagination is a powerful tool in creating new neural pathways and building new responses. Our imagination is something we all have access to; tap into the power you have within it and begin to see the difference it can make.

Using Mary's situation as an example, if she was putting her ATTENTION into changing her PERCEPTION at work for example, she may choose to imagine herself working at her desk with a 'Things To Action' list all ticked off and with a big smile on her face. Opening up this picture in her mind flags it up as a possible outcome to achieve, acting as an alternative focus from feeling that she never had enough time to do all that she wanted to.

"Imagination is more important than knowledge, for knowledge is limited whereas imagination embraces the entire world, stimulating progress, giving birth to evolution." **Albert Einstein**

Significance

We will be more likely to accept the concept of change if the idea is supported by a significant source, one which has particular relevance to our values or our world in some way. Opinions of others we respect can positively influence the significance and make it easier for our unconscious to accept the change.

The advertising world uses this concept in the art of persuading a consumer to buy something new.

We may well be swayed towards the idea of a new purchase if somebody we respect recommends it. How often have you been tempted to buy something because someone you admire is seen wearing or using it?

Have you ever noticed how your ideas might change when someone, who is significant to you makes a new suggestion? We give that suggestion far more credence because it has come from a significant source.

And then perhaps also, on the flip side, have you ever noticed how you can instantly dismiss an idea or concept from someone you don't value? Significance is such an important factor in influencing our unconscious processing.

Gathering guidance from 'significant' sources that support our chosen direction is another way to motivate and sustain change in our chosen direction. This may include speaking to others who have previously tread a similar path and gained helpful information to support you.

Perhaps it could mean connecting with a specialist who can share knowledgeable insights into that area. Or maybe it would be immersing yourself in an environment that will surround you with encouragement to support the change.

So, look outside of yourself too, for inspiration, knowledge and information that will help further improve the significance of the need to make the change you desire.

Emotions

Emotions and feelings form the foundation of our experiences; although an experience is made up of thoughts feelings and actions it's generally the feelings that will be at the centre of that experience.

For example, we may remember an image of a beautiful scene from a holiday but generally, it's the memory of how we felt as a result of it that is the best part of it!

And that's just the same for the 'not so pleasant' scenarios too. We may have a vivid picture in our mind of a horrible memory, but generally, it's the feeling that comes with it that brings the distress.

If we can change the emotion that is triggered by a situation then our PERCEPTION of it can be completely transformed. We can see it from a different place; and as a result, feel very different about it too.

Therefore, it's really important to connect with how you want to feel and, be mindful that this focus will take you in the direction of how you want to feel in the future; the more you practise the more natural that will become.

The power of our emotions is so significant that I have given a whole section of the APPEAR process over to Emotional Intention, and we will look at that in more detail in the next chapter.

Firstly though, we are going to look at an exercise that will help you shift your PERCEPTION of situations and begin to create a whole new reality for you.

Creating Your Reality

Using the principles of the ARISE concept we are going to create a new programme in your mind. We are going to create a Movie In Your Mind which will act as a template for future expectations, like creating a memory yet to come.

Movie In Your Mind Exercise

Now you have discovered that your imagination is a powerful tool in creating new neural programmes, it's time for you to use your imagination to create a new future for yourself.

We are going to create a Movie in Your Mind that you can use regularly to reinforce your intention of how you want things to be. This movie is a key component in training your Worry Warrior to anticipate new outcomes and so take away the need for it to jump into action.

Here's what to do:

- Identify what it is you want to change (from your AWARE work) and then decide how you think you would prefer things to be (from your PURPOSE for change).

- Then create an image in your mind of how things will be once you have left behind that unhelpful fear or negative expectation. Make it very clear in your mind, seeing as much detail as possible, including what you see, touch, smell, hear and feel, then make it into a Movie In Your Mind. Create this all into a short movie that captures all that you want things to be. When creating this Movie remember the principle of ARISE we discussed earlier.
- Each day find a quiet time when you can bring your ATTENTION into Your Movie In Your Mind and run through it.
- Practise it daily, the more you practise it the stronger it will become, REPETITION being a key factor in creating new programmes.
- Use your IMAGINATION to its full potential, creating an image of things yet to come, make it as vivid as you can and focus on the detail within the image.

- What influences of SIGNIFICANCE have supported your plan for change? How does this relate to you and your world in a positive way?
- And most importantly, draw your focus into how it feels to be there. Connecting with the EMOTION of it as this will be the glue that holds this image in place.
- Bring all of these elements together to make your Movie in Your Mind, run it through your mind every day and begin to see the changes it can bring.

Chapter Eight

EMOTIONAL INTENTION
Choose how you feel

As human beings, we are all able to experience a whole spectrum of emotions, good and bad and it's completely natural to experience a range of feelings at different times of our life.

However as previously mentioned, when our Worry Warrior is on high alert it's so much more likely that we will look out for the pitfalls, and problems, swaying us towards living life in a negative place.

Problems arise when we are not able to move past these difficult emotions; when the uncomfortable feelings become so intense, they dominate us. When the same uncomfortable emotions just keep on showing up this could be a message telling us that perhaps an unhelpful programme is being triggered.

Living life in a negative place can lead us to continually expect difficulties to arise for us and, as a result, we live life worrying about what has happened/is happening/will happen, this our Worry Warrior in full flow!

What we may not recognise though, is being in this place means we are looking out for the problems. **We Find What We Focus On**, so the more we look for difficulties, with our Worry Warrior believing that it is keeping us safe, the more difficulties we are likely to find.

By redirecting our attention in a different direction, we are much more likely to find a different outcome. By identifying how we want to feel, i.e., setting our Emotional Intention; we will be guiding our unconscious programming in the direction we want to go. It's like loading our mental 'satnav' with more detailed information about our desired destination. Our brain locks onto the emotions that we focus on and then will look out for opportunities to take us there.

The more time we can spend in a positive emotional state the less likely our Worry Warrior will be triggered and the calmer we will feel.

We can practise an exercise which will encourage our brain to focus on the positives around us, switching us to a happier place and calming our Worry Warrior. It's called Practicing Gratitude.

Practicing Gratitude

Think how it feels when something nice has been done for you, perhaps cooked a lovely meal, bought you a gift or maybe paid you a compliment.

We feel grateful and it feels good! This feeling of gratitude, it's at the top of the emotional scale, a good place, where most of us would choose to be.

If we take time out to look for the things we are grateful for each day, we are training our brain to look out for the positives, eventually resulting in us finding more of the good things than we did before.

Keeping a gratitude journal is one way that can make this work for you.

Noting down at least three things you are grateful for each day starts to draw your emotions into a positive place. Recognise the event and then connect it with the good feeling it brings.

These might only be small things and may even be things that in the past you may have taken for granted, such as a new flower opening in your garden or enjoying the comfort of a hot bath at the end of the day.

By regularly connecting with the good feeling that comes from noticing these things, it will ultimately become a habit that will bring more positivity into your day. The more you practise this, the more good things you will find around you. By pausing, and taking time to enjoy these things, you will be helping to re-programme your brain and settle your Worry Warrior into a better place.

There is a template of the Gratitude Action Sheet in Chapter Eleven *'Creating Your MindFit Map,'* which you can complete to help support your Gratitude practice.

Affirmations

Another way to support a shift of focus into positivity is to practise making Affirmations.

Affirmation means the act of confirming something to be true, so the more we affirm a positive emotional state, the more our brain will recognise this to be true. Here is an exercise that can help you create some positive statements that can trigger positive emotions and result in more positive outcomes.

Affirmation Exercise

Write down one or two statements that support positive emotions or beliefs that you would like to strengthen.

Keep these statements in the present tense, it brings that emotion to you in the here and now.

Review these affirmations regularly throughout your day, perhaps even saying them aloud too, then notice the differences this new practice brings you. By carrying out Gratitude Practice and

Affirmations each day you will be encouraging a shift into a positive mindset, looking for the good and as a result, finding more of it.

There is an Affirmation Action Sheet for you to complete in Chapter Eleven *'Creating Your MindFit Map.'*

Mary's Affirmations

Here is an example of the affirmations that support Mary in maintaining her Emotional Intention, these may vary from day to day depending on what her attention is focused on:

	I am……
Monday	I am confident in what I do.
Tuesday	I feel calm and happy.
Wednesday	I am getting done all that I want to .
Thursday	I am proud of what I achieve.
Friday	I feel secure about my finances.
Saturday	I am enjoying time to relax.
Sunday	I am excited about the week ahead.

Chapter Nine

ACTION Make it Happen

Wouldn't it be wonderful if we could wave a magic wand and everything fell into place, just as we want it to be? The outcomes I achieve with my clients are often described by them as magic; however, though it may feel like magic, there is a lot of commitment and action behind those results.

ACTIONS that Support Our Intention

After we have created our intention of how we want things to be, we must take action that supports our direction.

For each of the things you have identified that you want to change, rather than just waiting for an opportunity to arise that may mean you do something differently, you must commit to a specific action that will support that direction. For example, if we aim to improve confidence in our public speaking at work, then we might like to put ourselves forward to chair a meeting at work.

This supports our vision and allows us to put into practise all we have prepared ourselves for.

Always keep in mind, 'How can I make this vision a reality?' Then take action to bring it to life.

Other Actions That Keeps Our Worry Warrior in Check

Once we have followed the techniques to help shift our unhelpful programming, we will be less likely to find our Worry Warrior mode kicking into action, finding ourselves calmer and in a much happier place. However, it is still helpful to consider including activities in your life that will bring positive influences on your stress response to keep your Worry Warrior in check to maintain a healthy balance in your body and mind.

We won't cover the 'how to 'of these activities here but this mention serves to flag up things that you may like to include in your life.

Clear Your Mind, Free Your Body and Feed Your Soul

I categorise these ACTIONS into three areas as follows; Clear Your Mind, Free Your Body, Feed Your Soul.

I suggest that you consider including at least one ACTION from each section in your action list to ensure that you keep your Worry Warrior in check.

Clear Your Mind

In this section you might like to consider activities which will help to bring your mind back to a more relaxed place, such as meditation and relaxation techniques, both have been proven to have a positive influence on your emotional and physical wellbeing.

Meditation is a technique which teaches you to empty your mind by bringing your focus onto one thing, this may be a sound, a word, or perhaps becoming more aware of your body and the sensations you feel.

Many people prefer to begin with guided meditation which provides you with direction for your attention into a journey of relaxation.

The are many different examples of meditation available on YouTube and many helpful apps that make meditation an easy addition to your day.

Relaxation techniques including breathing exercises, or breathwork, are another way to bring you to a more comfortable place in your mind.

Both of these techniques will also have a positive influence on your body, as your mind clears your body relaxes too, and this also works in the reverse. If we ensure our body is moving as it is designed to, we are more likely to feel good.

Free Your Body

When our body can't move as it is designed to this can create stress within us. Many of our lives in the modern world are more sedentary than ever before and so we need to be mindful to include activities that move our bodies.

We gain emotional benefits from being physically active, stimulating endorphin release, our happy hormones, to help boost our mood.

Any physical activity we include is also an investment in our future physical health, keeping our muscles, joints and cardiovascular systems working at their best.

As our body ages, we need to put more work into keeping our body moving to maintain the same level of function; making exercise a habit at any age will reap the rewards at a later date.

When choosing a physical activity to follow it must be something that you enjoy.

Not everyone is cut out to be a gym bunny or a marathon runner, though if that suits you then that's great. You may prefer to choose something that suits who *you* are.

That may be taking a walk with a friend instead of meeting for coffee, dancing in your front room to your favourite tunes or jumping on a trampoline with your kids. So long as you are moving and enjoying the outcome that is the priority!

Pilates is an exercise I advocate for all my clients and I run regular Zoom classes so that it is accessible to everyone. This is both a body and mind activity as the mindful controlled exercises help to strengthen your muscles, improve flexibility and relax and refocus your mind. (See details in the Resources section)

Other activities such as Yoga and Tai Chi may also have similar effects. Take time out to include a *Free Your Body Activity* in your ACTIONs choosing something that suits you, fits in with your lifestyle, and that you enjoy.

Other elements to consider in this section also include, practising healthy eating, getting enough rest/sleep and ensuring appropriate hydration; all of which will contribute to maintaining optimum performance of our body and mind.

These elements are intrinsically linked to our stress levels. When eating sugar-rich processed foods our body gains very little nutritional value from them and the fluctuating blood sugar levels that arise from eating them can trigger our stress response. We may find ourselves more likely to eat this kind of food if we do feel stressed but as you can see, in the long run, it is more likely to increase our feelings of stress.

Changing eating habits can be a complicated process and sometimes the best results are achieved with more expert guidance in this area. Look to others to support you if you feel that you need more help in this area.

Sleep is another factor that we should consider, often being interrupted if we are stressed. However, in reverse, if we don't get enough sleep it can cause us to feel more stressed. If we take action to ensure we can get at least 7-8 hours of quality sleep a night, we are more likely to feel well.

Calming your Worry Warrior as you already are with the help of this book may bring the result of improved sleep, but we can support the outcome of a better night's sleep with several other actions too.

This may include scheduling a regular time to go to bed, rather than being distracted by TV, socialising or technology or setting an alarm for bedtime as well as for a morning call. Creating a bedtime routine where you can start to relax, such as reading, or a hot bath can be helpful too. Avoiding caffeine and alcohol for some hours before bedtime will also have a positive impact on sleep.

Recent research suggests that lack of sleep can be detrimental to our long-term health, with conditions such as Alzheimer's Disease, being linked to long-term sleep deprivation. The importance of sleep deprivation is sometimes overlooked and therefore needs to be given important consideration.

Our body is made up of 50% water so ensuring adequate daily hydration is vital for our body to function efficiently.

By the time we are thirsty, our body has already been dehydrated for a considerable time. As the body becomes dehydrated, it will trigger our stress response; our body recognising a shift away from our normal state of balance.

Regular water intake of approximately 2 litres a day will be another factor that can contribute to keeping us in a healthy and happy place.

Feed Your Soul

I'm sure everyone knows something that they like or would like to do that, *Feeds Their Soul*. This is something that brings you to a place where you feel you want to stay, where you feel in 'flow,' content and fulfilled.

However, very often it's these things that fall off the list of priorities when we are busy. Shift your attention to what you as an individual need, then you will see the benefits ripple out into your world in all sorts of ways.

Here are some important elements needed to *Feed Your Soul.*

Love and Connection

As human beings, connecting with others is part of our basic needs so take steps to maintain enjoyable connections with others; friends, family and others who have similar intents to you.

Connecting with nature is another way to bring ourselves to a calmer place, whether that's walking our dog, sitting in the park, climbing a mountain or just watching a nature documentary on TV.

Connecting with nature is something we don't always think about scheduling regularly in our week, but you'll see great benefits if you do.

Creativity

This doesn't necessarily mean you have to be artistic, as creativity just means creating something!

This could mean baking a cake, time with a mindfulness colouring book, or making an album of family photos. It could mean trying a new hobby such as pottery, joining a choir, learning to knit, or maybe even writing your own book!

All of these activities help calm your mind, at least they will do if you enjoy them; find something that works for you and bring more creativity into your life.

Fun Without Purpose

As children we instinctively know how to play and have fun, unfortunately as adults, life can get in the way and 'fun without purpose' or just having fun for the sake of fun, isn't given the importance it deserves.

Adult animals can be seen to engage in play frequently and it is seen as a joy of nature when we observe it.

Finding time for fun without any specific reason will bring a new dimension into your life, so think about what might tick this box for you.

It may already be something that you have included in the previous sections, or you may just decide to pepper the feeling of spontaneous fun into everyday activities; get imaginative and feel the benefits.

Spend some time considering these factors and create a list of ACTIONS you feel would be helpful to your journey. Use the *Actions I Can Take* Template in Chapter Eleven *Creating Your MindFit Map* to help you with this.

Remember that this is just a brainstorm of resources for you to refer to as you work through the process. You don't need to action all of them at once, so be imaginative in what you add to the lists, and then there will be plenty of suggestions for the future.

Chapter Ten

RESOURCES Support For Change

In this section, we focus on what and who could make the journey of Calming Your Worry Warrior, even easier for you.

This book is aimed at giving you some structure and techniques that can guide you along your way and, having read it, hopefully, you will feel more insightful and empowered to make the changes you want to.

On occasions however, you may find that a little bit of extra help can make that journey easier and reaching out for support may be something that you might like to consider.

There are a number of different reasons we may look for extra support.

- Perhaps it's feeling just too much of a challenge to do it all on your own.

- Maybe it seems there's lots to do and it's a bit too complicated and you're not sure where to start.
- Perhaps you would just like accountability and guidance to keep you on track.
- Or maybe it's just that you would like to get the job done so much more quickly.

Most of us work better with support and encouragement, so you may decide that sharing your journey with a trusted friend or loved one may be helpful to give you guidance and encouragement. Perhaps you may look for other resources from outside sources to help you along the way too.

You might decide you would like help in improving your fitness level to Free Your Body so joining a class or having personal training might be on your list.

It could be that help with healthy eating might be a priority for you, so look for a nutritional therapist to guide you, if this is the case.

Sometimes it can be a challenge to identify what needs to change or we may require additional intervention to make those changes. This is where working with a Therapist can help you on your journey to Calm Your Worry Warrior.

Choosing a Therapist to support your change in your mindset is a little like employing a personal trainer to help you get fit. You have an expert on hand who directs the process and can help identify exactly what's needed for you.

A therapist can use additional techniques and interventions to help you make the changes to your mindset more quickly and easily.

Hypnotherapy and BrainWorking Recursive Therapy

As a Therapist I feel in a privileged position to help my clients make fast-acting and permanent changes to their mindset, helping them to shift old unhelpful patterns of belief and expectations using a number of different techniques, including Hypnotherapy and Brain Working Recursive Therapy.

Hypnotherapy is a powerful tool for facilitating positive change in mindset by tapping into the subconscious mind. Contrary to common misconceptions, hypnosis isn't about relinquishing control of your mind, but rather about harnessing it more effectively. Through guided relaxation and focused attention, hypnotherapy enables individuals to access deeper layers of their psyche, where ingrained thought patterns and behaviours reside. By rewiring neural pathways, hypnosis helps to reframe perspectives, overcome limiting beliefs, and foster more constructive habits. It's a collaborative process between the therapist and the client, aimed at empowering individuals to unlock their inner potential and achieve lasting transformation in their mental landscape. BrainWorking Recursive Therapy ® (BWRT®) is another powerful technique that I use.

It is a modern therapeutic approach designed to help individuals overcome a variety of psychological challenges by targeting the root causes of their issues and creating new patterns of thinking, feeling, and behaviour by effectively rewiring the brain's neural pathways.

Both of these techniques access the brain's natural capacity for neuroplasticity, which means re-wiring new neural pathways.

In doing so, we can change our expectations and beliefs and break free from negative thought cycles and emotional triggers.

These technique helps me support my clients to reach their goals in a simple and effortless way, with them often reporting amazement at how different they feel afterwards; not just with the problem they sought help for, but in many other ways within their life too.

We may feel nervous to ask for extra help as it can feel challenging to share our vulnerabilities. However, facing our vulnerabilities is one of the strongest things we can do, so if needs be, be bold and reach out for help to make sure that you realise your dreams.

Use the *Resources Action Sheet* (included in Chapter Eleven) to help you focus on what support might facilitate your journey to Calm Your Worry Warrior.

Chapter Eleven

CREATING YOUR MINDFIT MAP
Your Personal Guide to Calm Your Worry Warrior

So far, we have looked at several different exercises that will help you become more focused on what might be triggering your Worry Warrior and have shown you some techniques that could help you calm it.

Here is a review of the activities we have discussed so far. If you haven't had a chance to complete them yet, take time out now to work through them one at a time. Remember to look back to the previous chapters for more detailed guidance on how to carry them out. You can make copies of each exercise template so that you can repeat again at a later date.

Activity sheets

Aware:

Worry Warrior Quiz

Have a look at this list and see how many of the following questions apply to you.

1. I often feel anxious and find I am often worrying about what has happened or might happen in the future.
2. I question my decisions, am I doing the right thing
3. I find it difficult to get myself out of a low mood.
4. I am often worried about what other people think of me.
5. I find myself getting angry and find it difficult to control this.
6. I feel overwhelmed with all that I need to do.
7. I place other people's needs above my own.
8. I feel stuck and don't know how to change the situation.
9. I find myself acting in a way I later regret.
10. I find that there are often things would love to do but somehow, I can't.
11. I find it hard to relax, my brain never wants to switch off.
12. I have ongoing pain that restricts what I can do on occasions.
13. I have several allergies or sensitivities.
14. I frequently suffer from migraines.
15. I have been diagnosed with an autoimmune problem.
16. I have to be careful what I eat as I am prone to irritable bowel symptoms.

How many of these did you tick? If you agreed with *any* of these statements it could mean that your Worry Warrior is getting in your way of living life to the full. The more you have ticked the more likely it is that Calming your Worry Warrior Within will have a positive impact on your life.

Take note of these statements and so you can record any of these in the AWARE section on your MindFit Map, (see further into the chapter for this template).

Wheel of Life Exercise

On the wheel, that is divided up into sections, score each section from 1 to 10, with 1 being where your Worry Warrior is most active and you feel most stressed or anxious, and with 10 being the happiest score, when everything feels as it should be.

What we are aiming for is balance across the whole wheel, if particular areas are much lower than others then these are the areas to focus on initially.

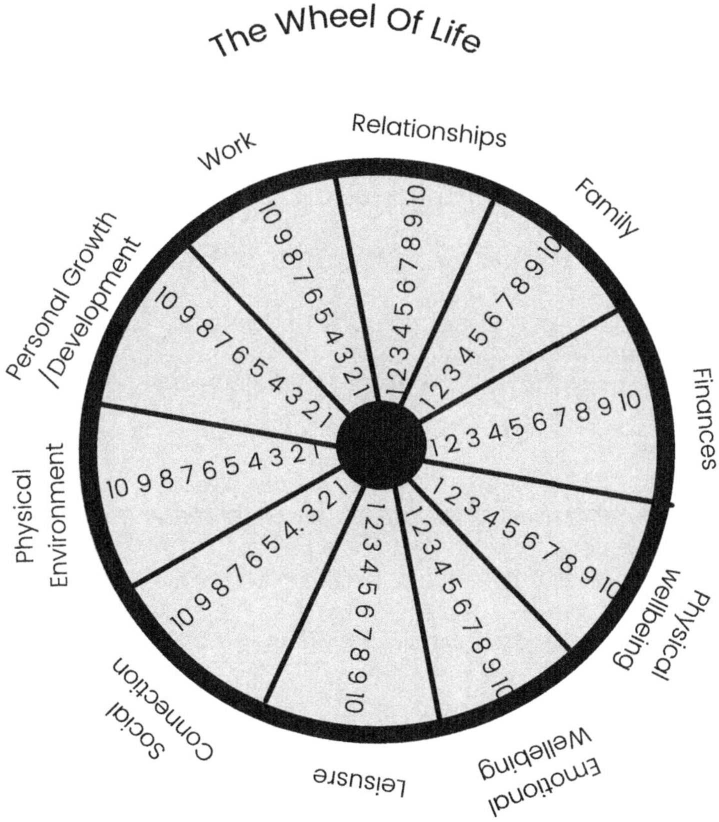
The Wheel Of Life
Relationships
Family
Finances
Physical Wellbeing
Emotional Wellbeing
Leisusre
Social Connection
Physical Environment
Personal Growth /Development
Work
1 2 3 4 5 6 7 8 9 10

For any area that you have scored lower than a 6, think about what the challenges are and review the reasons you have given it this score, write this in the relevant box on the form.

Now look at this area and think about any unhelpful beliefs that may be connected to this area and record them also on the form.

It's important to reflect on what is good and working well in your life too; hopefully, you will have had time to think about this too in this exercise.

For any of the sections that score higher than a 6 spend some time reflecting on why this area feels good, what's going well here and what are the beliefs attached to this?

It's helpful to recognise what's working well and recognise our success too.

If you haven't scored any sections above 6, that's ok. This gives you an understanding that there is some work to do across the board. The good thing is you are ready to make some changes and you are committed to finding out how to do that.

If it feels a bit uncomfortable looking at the lists of negative things showing up in your life, try to see what you have uncovered as a positive.

This is only a reflection of where you are today; not where you want to be. Remember that exposing our vulnerabilities is ultimately empowering, it is the first step to making change.

Completing this exercise shows your intent to change and that is one of the most powerful ingredients in making a positive difference.

Area of Wheel of Life	Score 1-10	Reasons for Score Why does this feel good/ what is the challenge? What is/ isn't working well?	Unhelpful beliefs and expectations What am I afraid might happen?
Work A job that meets your purpose			
Relationship A relationship that meets your individual needs			
Family Balance within your family relationships			
Finances Feeling confident and secure around your money			
Physical Wellbeing Feeling fit and healthy			
Emotional Wellbeing Feeling happy and content			
Leisure Fun without purpose			
Social connection Sharing friendships			
Physical Environment Living and working conditions			

Any other difficult events	Unhelpful beliefs or expectations associated with these events	How is that showing up in my life?

Purpose:

Living By Our Values

- On the list on the next page, highlight the dot next to each word that resonates with you. Don't think about it too much, just go with your first gut reaction to each word.
- Then go through the words you have marked and circle 5 of these words that feel most important to you.
- Write these five words (in order) in the CORE section below.
- Then return to your list of those you highlighted, and repeat with the next 5 most important words, write these into the GROWTH section below.
- Repeat with the next 5 most important words and then write them in the FLOURISH Section.

The CORE values are the most fundamental to our basic happiness.

The GROWTH values will further support your enjoyment in life.

The FLOURISH values bring a higher fulfillment to your life.

Values:

*Acceptance *Control *Humour *Privacy *Success

*Achievement *Creativity * Imagination *Productivity

*Teaching *Adventure

*Equality *Independence *Promotion

*Prospects *Teamwork * Altruism *Status

*Excellence *Influence *Reaching potential

*Tolerance * Ambition * Excitement *Intellect

*Recognition *Tradition *Appreciation *Expertise

*Intuition *Respect *Travel *Authenticity

*Fairness *Justice *Responsibility *Trust *Authority

*Faith *Kindness * Results * Variety *Autonomy

*Fame *Leadership *Risk taking *Winning

*Balance *Family * Learning * Romance *Wisdom

*Beauty *Fast pace * Love *Routine

*Zest for life *Belonging *Financial rewards

*Loyalty *Safety *Certainty *Focus *Making a difference

*Security * Challenge *Freedom

*Nurturing *Self Expression *Collaboration *Fun *Order *Service

*Commitment *Happiness *Passion *Sharing (Continued...)

*Compassion *Health * Perfection *Spirituality *Connection

*Helping Others *Personal Growth

*Stability *Contribution *Honesty *Power

CORE:	GROWTH:	FLOURISH:
1	1	1
2	2	2
3	3	3
4	4	4
5	5	5

Purpose for Change Activity Template

Area of Wheel of Life	*What will the change mean for you? What are you able to do now that you have made a change? What will be different?*
Work A job that meets your purpose	
Relationship A relationship that meets your individual needs	
Family Balance within your family relationships	
Finances Feeling confident and secure around your money	
Physical Wellbeing Feeling fit and healthy	
Emotional Wellbeing Feeling happy and content	
Leisure Fun without purpose	
Social Connection Sharing friendships	
Physical Environment Living and working conditions	
Personal Growth/ Development Fulfilling your potential	

Perception: Activity Sheet Identify any unhelpful fears or beliefs and see if you can change your view on this by looking at the evidence around this. (There is more help on how to do this in Chapter Seven.)

Area of Wheel of Life	**What evidence can you find that proves a different perceptive?**
Work	
Relationship	
Family	
Finances	
Physical Wellbeing	
Emotional Wellbeing	
Leisure	
Social Connection	
Physical Environment	
Personal Growth/ Development	

Movie In Your Mind Activity

Now you have discovered that your imagination is a powerful tool in creating new neural programmes, it's time for you to use your imagination to create a new future for yourself.

You are going to create a Movie in Your Mind that you can use regularly to reinforce your intention of how you want things to be.

This movie is a key component in training your Worry Warrior to anticipate new outcomes and so change the need for it to jump into action.

- Create an image in your mind of how things will be once you have left behind that unhelpful fear or negative expectation.
- Make it very clear in your mind, seeing as much detail as possible, and make the image as vivid as you can.
- Each day find a quiet time when you can bring your ATTENTION in this exercise and run through the Movie in Your Mind.
- The more times you practise it the stronger it will become - REPETITION being the tool that makes it stick.
- Use your IMAGINATION to its full potential, creating an image of things yet to come.
- Focus on the SIGNIFICANCE this has to you.
- Connect strongly with the EMOTIONS and feelings that come from being in that place. Recognise how it feels as if this is a reality for you now.
- Bring all of these elements together to make your Movie in Your Mind.

Emotional Intention:

GRATITUDE PRACTICE

Choosing gratitude as a habit will bring more positivity to your day.

Note down at least three things you are grateful for each day. Reflect on the event, and why you are grateful for it. Then connect with the good feeling that brings.

These might only be small things, sometimes things that in the past you may have taken for granted, such as a new flower opening in your garden or enjoying the comfort of a hot bath at the end of the day.

The more you practise this, the more of the good things you will find around you.

By pausing and taking time to enjoy these things you will be helping to re-programme your brain and settle your Worry Warrior into a better place.

	I am so grateful for	Because......
Monday		
Tuesday		
Wednesday		
Thursday		
Friday		
Saturday		
Sunday		

AFFIRMATIONS

Affirmation means the act of confirming something to be true, so the more we affirm our emotions the more our brain will recognise this to be true.

Each day write down one or two statements that support positive emotions or beliefs that you would like to strengthen. Repeat these statements in your mind, regularly throughout your day, or if you want more effect say them aloud.

	My affirmations e.g., I am confident and calm
Monday	
Tuesday	
Wednesday	
Thursday	
Friday	
Saturday	
Sunday	

Next Step - Create your MindFit Map

You may find there is a lot of information that you have gathered together here, and that's a good thing, the more information you have the more you understand, though perhaps it may feel a little confusing as to what to do with it all!

So, the next step in your journey to Calm Your Worry Warrior is to compile your MindFit Map. In doing so you will have a clear step-by-step plan to support you on your journey. Make copies of the template and use as many as you need, one for each area that you wish to create change in (see next page for your template).

Take each element you wish to work on and apply the APPEAR process to create your MindFit Map, which will be your guide for change.

Use the MindFit Map template to record your journey. Use the in-formation that you have already identified to help you formulate your answers to each section.

MINDFIT MAP TEMPLATE
AWARE What unhelpful fears, beliefs or expectations have you now recognised are getting in the way of how you want to think feel or act?
PURPOSE What benefits will arise from changing these? What will that mean to you and how you live your life?
PERCEPTION See these things from a different perspective, create an image of how you could see things from a different place.
EMOTIONAL INTENTION How will you be feeling now the situation has changed?
ACTIONS What actions are you taking to support/implement these changes?
RESOURCES What help or support will ensure you make these changes? Where will you find this?

Refer back to each previous chapter for more details of each section, but here is an overview for each part of the APPEAR process.

AWARE

In this section select and record one element that you have become aware of that is getting in your way. This may be an unhelpful belief or fear, for example. Use the information you discovered from the Wheel of Life exercise to help you identify this.

PURPOSE for Change

Here, make notes of the purpose of this change for you. How will life be different for you? What will you be doing as a result of leaving behind those old patterns? What will that mean for you?

Also, in this section, include any relevant values that you will be meeting by making this change.

Remember to focus on what you *do want* rather than what you *don't*. Keep it positive and in the present tense.

PERCEPTION

In this section note down the evidence you have found that allows you to see things from a different place.

Create a Movie In Your Mind of how things will be once you have made the change, give it a name and outline it in this section. Remember the rules of ARISE.

EMOTIONAL INTENTION

Now think about how you will feel once you have let go of those unhelpful patterns and can live life as you want to. How will you be feeling in that Movie in Your Mind? State what feelings and emotions you will notice as a result of the changes. Write down any affirmations that will be helpful to you.

ACTION

In this section make some commitments to regular activities you will include in your day that you know will help Calm your Worry Warrior.

Include in this, Movie in Your Mind practise, your Affirmation and Gratitude practice, and any other ACTIONS that support change in this specific area.

Give yourself clear parameters for the actions, including when you will start and when will you take the action.

RESOURCES

In this section make notes of any support that may help you reach your goals more easily, then reach out to find it.

Mary's MindFit Map

To give you an idea of how the MindFit Map can help, here is an example from Mary. In addition to the therapy, we did together, she used her MindFit Map to help her change the unhelpful belief that she was responsible for everyone's happiness, which had been proving to be a real burden on her.

MARY'S MINDFIT MAP
AWARE *What unhelpful fears, beliefs or expectations have you now recognised are getting in the way of how you want to think feel or act?*
I am afraid of upsetting others. I feel it is my responsibility to make sure that everyone else is happy. The weight of this responsibility means I always feel under pressure and never have enough time to do everything.
PURPOSE *What benefits will arise from changing these? What will that mean to you and how you live your life?*
I have sufficient time to do all that I want to do so I feel confident in getting done all that I want to. I am more focused, productive, and motivated and as a result, I enjoy work more. I have time to enjoy hobbies.
PERCEPTION *See these things from a different perspective, create an image of how you could see things from a different place.*
I recognise that my children are capable of doing more and I should trust their capabilities as a result I will feel calmer at home. I can support my family members in finding happiness, but it isn't solely my responsibility. Others can support me too. My Movie in My Mind is of me having fun with the family feeling relaxed and laughing. It's called Fun Time!
EMOTIONAL INTENTION *How will you be feeling now the situation has changed?*
I feel happy, confident and calm. I feel lighter and freer.
ACTIONS *What actions are you taking to support/implement these changes?*
I take time out for myself each day, finding time to read and have fun with the family. Each day I practise my Gratitude and Affirmations before I go to bed. I drink at least 2 litres of water each day and have bought a new water bottle to remind me. I exercise 3 times a week but have also included a weekly Pilates class. I practise my Mind Movie every day first thing in the morning before everyone else gets up.
RESOURCES *What help or support will ensure you make these changes? Where will you find this?*
I have asked my family to respect the time I need to do things for myself and they are supporting me in taking time to do things that are important to me. I have booked an online Pilates Class.

Using Your MindFit Map

Now that you have created your MindFit Map follow it and turn your plan into reality, make sure to put your intention into action.

Make it a live document, put it up somewhere you can see it regularly, this will act as a reminder to you of where you are heading and how you will get there.

Remember 'Practice makes Permanent' so make following your MindFit Map a daily habit to keep you on your journey to calm your Worry Warrior.

Once you feel you are comfortable with one element, move on to deal with the next issue and create another MindFit Map.

Once you have made a habit of using your MindFit Map you will find yourself using the APPEAR process for any challenge that presents itself to you.

It's great to hear feedback from clients who are using this. They say, 'I looked at the issue, (AWARE). Then thought about the benefits if I were to change it. I asked myself do I change the situation or the way I feel about it? (PURPOSE). Then I went on to change my perspective on it (PERCEPTION). I took action and asked 'XYZ' to help me with this too. Wow. What a difference that process has made for me when anything challenging arises.'

Take some time to become familiar with The APPEAR process. Every single one of us deserves to discover that person who has been hiding behind our Worry Warrior.

You have taken the first step... now continue the journey to calm your Worry Warrior.....and to allow your true self to APPEAR!

"Maybe the journey isn't so much about becoming anything. Maybe it's about un-becoming everything that isn't really you, so you can be who you were meant to be in the first place."

Paulo Coelho

Final Note

I hope you have enjoyed reading this book and have found the information and resources helpful for you to uncover and Calm Your Worry Warrior.

I hope it has given you the confidence that it is possible to change and, that you have discovered that there is a way to do that. Please reach out to me with any questions or comments you may have about the book. I would also love to hear about your success. Sharing your success inspires others, so let them know what a difference it can make, to Calm Your Worry Warrior.

For more information about the services I offer, including individual therapy sessions, workshops, Pilates Classes, and Hypnotherapy Diploma training, please check out my website: at Bodymind-solutions.co.uk or visit via the QR code.

You can also connect with me via social media: https://linktr.ee/Sandrabodymindsolutions

Acknowledgments

Firstly, a massive thank you to Karen Stanley of *Mabel & Stanley* Publishing for your expert guidance and support (and red pen!) in the editing and publishing of this book. You have inspired and motivated me to bring to print, the book that I had swimming around in my head for so long; thank you, Karen!

Thank you too, to the clients who have put their trust in me to make a difference in your lives. Without you, there would be no story. With each client I work with, I too grow and learn, gaining more knowledge to share with others.

An enormous thank you to my family. Tim, my husband, for your amazing love and for always having my back. My daughters, Sophie and Beth for your wonderful love and support on my journey as a working Mum. For Mum and Dad for always being there and saying, 'You can achieve anything you want to.'

And thank you, to all those I have met along the way, too many to name, who have inspired, motivated, and supported me. I know your valuable insights have allowed me to share more wisdom and knowledge with others, so thank you too.

About the Author

Sandra Hughes brings over 35 years of rich experience in healthcare, including work as a Clinical Hypnotherapy Practitioner and Trainer, Chartered Physiotherapist and Pilates Instructor. Throughout her career, she has been dedicated to inspiring positive change in others, impacting the lives of countless clients and helping them achieve happier and healthier lifestyles.

Sandra lives in Hythe, Kent with her husband Tim, and has two adult daughters.

Beyond her professional endeavours, Sandra finds joy in lifelong learning, exploring the outdoors with their dog, indulging in invigorating swims in the sea, staying active at the gym, spending time creating things at her sewing machine, and delving into the pages of captivating books. Her multifaceted interests reflect her vibrant spirit and unwavering commitment to personal growth and well-being.

BodyMind Solutions
the training academy
HYPNOTHERAPY•PSYCHOLOGY•
PERSONAL DEVELOPMENT

If this book has inspired you to help others make positive change then our Clinical Hypnotherapy Practitioner Diploma could be for you!

We would love you to join us on the transformative journey of our Hypnotherapy Practitioner Diploma programme at BodyMind Solutions Training Academy. Our comprehensive curriculum offers you a multitude of benefits. Through expert instruction and hands-on experience, you'll gain a deep understanding of hypnotherapy techniques, enabling you to facilitate profound positive changes in your clients' lives.

Our emphasis on practical skills development, coupled with theoretical knowledge, equips you with the confidence and competence to excel in the field of Hypnotherapy.

Join us to unlock your potential and embark on a rewarding career in Hypnotherapy. For more details go to:

Bodymind-solutiuons.co.uk/training-academy or use the QR code below.

Printed in Great Britain
by Amazon

48216125R00086